Arise!:
The Devotional for Warrior Wives

Dominique M. McGee

Copyright © 2018 Dominique M. McGee

All rights reserved. No part of this publication may be reproduced, distributed, or transmitted in any form or by any means, including photocopying, recording, or other electronic or mechanical methods, without the prior written permission of the publisher, except in the case of brief quotations embodied in critical reviews and certain other noncommercial uses permitted by copyright law.

Unless otherwise indicated, all scripture quotations are taken from the HOLY BIBLE, NEW INTERNATIONAL VERSION®.

Scripture quotations marked NEW INTERNATIONAL VERSION are taken from the HOLY BIBLE, NEW INTERNATIONAL VERSION®. Copyright 1973, 1978, 1984 by International Bible Society. Used by permission of Zondervan. All rights reserved.

Scripture quotations marked THE MESSAGE are taken from THE MESSAGE. Copyright © 1993, 1994, 1996, 2000, 2001, 2002. Used by permission of NavPress Publishing Group.

ISBN-13: 978-0-578-43114-7

Cover Design: Design Sheba
Editor: Cheryce F. Thompson

To keep up with updates follow us on social media @arisethedevotional.

DEDICATION

I dedicate this devotional to Marc and Rhonda who gave Corey and me the most valuable gems of marriage.

CONTENTS

Introduction	1
Day 1: Awaken	2
Day 2: Prework: Wholeness and Deliverance	4
Day 3: You Are Not Alone	6
Day 4: Comfort	8
Day 5: Grace	11
Day 6: Betrayal	14
Day 7: Forgiveness	16
Day 8: Mediation	19
Day 9: Empowerment	22
Day 10: His Sins	24
Day 11: Sacrifice	26
Day 12: Self-Care	28
Day 13: Worship	30
We Have Arrived Poem	32

Day 14: Comparison	33
Day 15: Gender Roles	36
Day 16: Putting In Work	38
Day 17: Distractions	40
Day 18: Sex	43
Day 19: Submission	45
Day 20: Image	47
Day 21: Finances	49
Day 22: Affirmations	51
Day 23: Sweet As A Honeybee	53
Day 24: Freedom	55
I See You Poem	57

KNOW THE DIFFERENCE

Any form of abuse is not love, know the difference. For more information please visit The National Domestic Violence Hotline at www.thehotline.org or call 1.800.799.SAFE (7233).

INTRODUCTION

"So may all your enemies perish, Lord! But may all who love you be like the sun when it rises in its strength" (Judges 5:31a, New International Version). Deborah, a prophetess and judge who lead Israel, spoke these words. She settled disputes under the palm tree called "Deborah" and many came to her for wise counsel.

What we as wives can learn from Deborah is to arise. Too many marriages have failed and it is time for us to arise and fight for our marriages. Marriage is one of God's most beautiful gifts. However, no marriage is perfect and hard times will come. In times of hardship, use this devotional to comfort you, to remind you of your purpose as a wife, to help you arise with strength and to remember the beauty of your marriage.

DAY 1: AWAKEN

Wake up, wake up, Deborah! Wake up, wake up, break out in song! Arise, Barak! Take captive your captives... - Judges 5:12

Up! Arise! Go forth! These are the commands that Deborah gave Barak when they fought against Sisera's army. The enemy hates marriage and he has waged a war against us. Wives, it's time to arise and fight for our marriages. We are mighty women of God and He has equipped us to fight against the enemy. God has covered you, embraced you and breathed life into you. Take the time now to prophesy over your husband and speak life into your marriage.

Dear God,

I speak life into my marriage. My marriage is not over. My weeping has endured for this night, but I am now moving into my season of joy (Psalm 30:5). I was only a seed in the beginning, but after the storm, I am growing into a beautiful lily. I will dance in the presence of God. There will be peace in my marriage. I have obeyed Your command and I will arise.

Amen.

DAY 2:
PREWORK: WHOLENESS AND DELIVERANCE

He is before all things, and in him all things hold together. - Colossians 1:17

I've heard so many newly married wives say, "I have found my other half, he completes me." While this sounds romantic, it could be the root problem in some marriages. Long before marriage comes, God's desire is for his children to be whole. Completeness comes from God, not from man. "May God himself, the God who makes everything holy and whole, make you holy and whole, put you together - spirit, soul, and body - and keep you fit for the coming of our Master, Jesus Christ" (I Thess. 5:23, The Message).

Wholeness is about knowing who you are and being

set free from all the baggage that is hindering you from being confident. What do you need to rise up from? Are you still hurting from what happened to you in the past? Are you bruised from previous relationships? Are you suffering from unforgiveness? Were you or are you happy in your singleness season or are you basing your happiness on a "perfect man?" Before marriage, these are the issues from which we need to be free. It also isn't too late for deliverance during marriage.

The Merriam-Webster dictionary describes the verb "deliver" as "to set free or to hand over, surrender". Before moving forward, evaluate yourself to find what you need healing from. Let go of that personal baggage because it will be harming to your marriage. Spend some time focusing on your own wholeness. Get prayer, seek counseling and get delivered.

Dear God,

I am Your daughter first, before I am a wife. Make me whole so that I will not need a man to complete me. Heal and deliver me from past hurts, so that I will not bring them into my marriage. I am beautiful, I am confident and I will rise up because I am free and complete.

Amen.

DAY 3:
YOU ARE NOT ALONE

But God demonstrates his own love for us in this: While we were still sinners, Christ died for us. - Romans 5:8

I remember the days we'd get up for marriage counseling and I'd say to my husband, "Oh yeah, they are going to tell you about yourself, just watch." Man, oh, man I'd start off so happy to go, hurrying up and pulling up my socks, throwing on my hat and coat and happily prancing out of the door. But, when I got there, I'd feel like the finger I was pointing at him became ten fingers pointing right back at me. In those moments I would feel so alone.

I remember thinking, "What about me? What about how I feel?" While what my counselors told me about myself was not wrong, I still felt the need to be heard and comforted. But the scripture says, "Blessed are those who mourn, for they will be comforted" (Matthew 5:4). Remember that you are not the only wife who is going through and feeling misunderstood. All of us have our own stories. Don't be ashamed. Cry out to God and express to Him your thoughts and frustrations. What usually works for me in those times is writing letters to God or writing affirmations to myself. Know that God understands us in our nighttime hour and He will carry us into the morning. You are not alone. Arise.

Dear God,

Comfort me. Thank you for reminding me that I am not alone. At this time I feel misunderstood. Remind me to trust You when I am weak. Strengthen me. Remind me that I don't have to be perfect. Help me to see myself. Help me to not judge my husband, but to see him in the way that You see him. Help me to vent my frustrations in a healthy way. Build me up so that I can build up my husband. Mend the broken pieces. Help me arise.

Amen.

DAY 4: COMFORT

Because of the Lord's great love, we are not consumed, for his compassions never fail. They are new every morning. - Lamentations 3:22-23a

Picture this: Tears wetting up my face and I'm saying, "What do I do, God? I am beyond tired of being in this place. I need you to wrap me in Your arms, God. But, I won't stop pressing until I feel You near me. Ignite Your fire, God! I cannot do this alone."

What do you think was happening here? On that night, my husband and I had just gotten into another argument. At first, I wanted to be comforted by him, but then I had to realize that he is just a man, he is not God. Our husbands do not deserve the pressure of comforting us every time we are hurting. Let's be real. If we are both in a heated argument, what is the likelihood of him stopping the conversation to comfort you? Did you stop and comfort him?

It took me a long time and consistency to get to the place of pressing into God's presence when I needed comfort. But honestly, my marriage became a lot easier once I stopped relying on my husband to be my superhero. I wanted him to read my mind, always know what to say and magically cater to my every need. When he wouldn't, I'd be furious and think, "He is so selfish. He doesn't love me and he doesn't know how to cater to my needs." How foolish of me to rely on my man to be my God!

Wives, we have to look to the hills from which comes our help. Press into His presence. Psalm 61: 3 says, "For you [God] have been my refuge, a strong tower against the foe. Remember that we are fighting a war against the enemy, not our husbands. Man is made after God's image, so He is the one we go to who will change our husband's heart.

Dear God,

Do not let me find fault with my husband at this time. O God, I need healing from You. Do not let me seek healing from my husband, but lead me to the rock that is higher than both of us. Although my enemies are against me, help me see that my husband is not my enemy. Dress us so that he and I can fight this war against Satan together. I speak over my mental stability right now in Jesus' name. My husband is not to blame. I stomp on the head of Satan right now. I am strong. My husband loves me and he is not my enemy. In Jesus' name I pray.

Amen.

DAY 5: GRACE

God is love. - 1John 4:8b

One of the most valuable lessons I learned in pre-marriage counseling was that God's grace was made sufficient for me. Dictionary.com defines grace as the "freely given, unmerited favor and love of God." Although we mocked, condemned, spit on and whipped Jesus to the ground, He still got up, carried His cross and died for us because He loves us.

This is how we usually see God's grace. After we sin, we go to God and sincerely repent. But most times, after we repent, we still mess up and repeat the same sin that we wholeheartedly asked forgiveness for. And what does God do? He STILL forgives us. If marriage was made to model Christ's love for the church, why shouldn't we show grace to our husbands?

So how do we show grace to our husbands? When Jesus was in the garden of Gethsemane, His heart was sorrowful because He knew He had to die. He fell to His face and transparently cried out to God. The same way Christ was transparent with God, is the same way we need to go to God when our husbands have offended us. This is the first step in showing grace.

The second step is obedience. Jesus asked God, "My Father, if it is possible may this cup be taken from me. Yet not as I will, but as you will" (Matthew 26:39). As wives, God called us to love our husbands and love is grace. So, be obedient and show your husband the grace of God. Who are we to say that our husbands don't deserve our love? I had to realize that my husband is not perfect and marriage was a new experience for him. He is not going to get everything right. He may do good in my eyes one day and then fall the next day. But, he still deserves grace because I am not perfect either.

Dear God,

I just want to say thank You. When I thought it was going to be impossible for my marriage to work, You proved me wrong. You took my husband's heart and You smoothed it out. You changed his worldview and You turned it around for Your glory. You molded Your son. I am grateful to be Your daughter, Messiah. Thank You for Your grace, for it is sufficient for me.

Amen.

DAY 6: BETRAYAL

May the God of hope fill you with all joy and peace as you trust in him, so that you may overflow with hope by the power of the Holy Spirit. - Romans 15:13

Trust in a marriage is such a beautiful entity. God designed trust to enhance the relationship between husband and wife. There is nothing wrong with trusting your husband wholeheartedly. I thought that my husband could do no wrong. But, one day he did do something to hurt me and compromise my trust. I felt betrayed because he was my best friend and a person I greatly trusted. To date, this is one of the toughest issues that our marriage has had to overcome. It may sound crazy, but I'm glad this happened to me. I had to be reminded that my husband is not perfect and grace is always needed. I am also grateful for this experience because it taught me hope.

Wives, if there is love in your marriage, I want you to know that there is hope after betrayal. Whether you or your husband lied, cheated, or stole, whatever the offense, there is hope. After repentance, God makes all things new. Thinking back to that time, I wish I had remembered this scripture, "But those who hope in the Lord will renew their strength" (Isaiah 40:31a). Put your trust in God and He will mend your broken heart. I promise God will strengthen your marriage.

Dear God,

I feel hurt and my heart is heavy. My spirit feels like shattered glass. Why did this have to happen in my marriage? God, I just pray that You lift me up. Remind me that neither of us is perfect. Teach me to have grace for and hope in our marriage. God, You have tied us together and we shall not be broken. Mend my heart and calm my spirit so that I may forgive and continue to love my husband unconditionally. Help me show him Your Godly grace. God, rebuild the trust between us. Show me that as long as I put my trust in You, You will begin to make things new. We are bound together.
Amen.

DAY 7:
FORGIVENESS

Then Peter came to Jesus and asked, "Lord, how many times shall I forgive my brother when he sins against me? Up to seven times?" Jesus answered, "I tell you not seven times, but seventy-seven times." - Matthew 18:21-22

Trust me when I say, I know what it feels like to go through hurts and trials with my husband. There were times I thought I would never forgive him. But, what I had to learn was that I had to forgive him so that I could be set free. "For if you forgive other people when they sin against you, your heavenly Father will also forgive you. But if you do not forgive others their sins, your Father will not forgive your sins" (Matthew 6:14-15). This means that you must forgive for your soul to be at peace. While I was in a state of unforgiveness, I was bitter, prideful and depressed. But, once I decided to forgive (which took the strength of God), God forgave me and freed me from those negative feelings about myself and toward my husband. Understand that forgiveness is a choice. I chose to forgive my husband and to love him. It was hard for me to do, but once I forgave, I stopped holding the offenses over his head. It was like it never happened, because love holds no record of wrongdoing. So, wives, don't allow unforgiveness to seep into your heart and damage you like a dirty oil spill. Talk to a counselor or therapist, someone who can hold you accountable to forgive and conquer your hurt. Be renewed and free to rise up in your marriage.

Dear God,

I pray that You give me the heart to forgive my husband. Remind me that he is just a man with imperfections, just as I am a woman with imperfections. Lord, teach me how to not stunt my own spiritual and marital growth because I have not learned how to forgive. Teach me to make Your ways my own and show me how You forgive me. I will be obedient and show love and forgiveness to my husband as

You have shown me. Set me free, O God, from bitterness and pridefulness. Prepare my heart to forgive and rise up. Amen.

DAY 8: MEDIATION

"This is my Son, whom I love; with him I am well pleased. Listen to him!" - Matthew 17:5b

God blessed Deborah with many Godly characteristics. Because she had a strong relationship with God, He blessed her with wisdom. As a judge, she settled many disputes. Although not explicitly mentioned, wisdom is a key aspect of this devotional. It is imperative that we have wisdom. We need to know when there is a third party needed to mediate our marriage.

Marriage is a covenant. I think of it as a binding contract that cannot be broken. Life happens, and we go through things with our husbands. The enemy uses that time to step in between our marriages and pull us away from our husbands. When we are constantly fighting with each other or if situations worsen, that is when we need a mediator.

The role of the mediator is to hear both sides of the disagreement as an outsider looking in, so that they can give more sound advice. In my opinion, the best mediators for marriages is a person or married couple who believes in the same biblical foundation of marriage as you and your husband. Seek God while finding a mediator. It should be someone with a good reputation, who you trust. This ensures that the extremely personal matters of your marriage remain private.

One of the biggest mistakes you can make, that could possibly set your marriage up for failure, is not having wise counsel. Another thing that I had to learn in my marriage is that sometimes individual professional help is needed. It helped me release all of the baggage that was there before my marriage. Please do not feel embarrassed to seek some help. The Word says, "Where no counsel is, the people fall: but in the multitude of counselors there is safety" (Proverbs 11:14). Please don't let the enemy get in between your marriage. Instead, seek help and keep your marriage on a solid rock.

Dear God,

I pray for Your Godly wisdom. I pray that You continue to keep my husband and I bound together by staying in the center of our marriage. Help me to put aside my pride and seek the help that we need. Please lead us to find Christian counselors to help us see outside of ourselves and our mistakes. I pray that You remove all the people and influences from marriage, that mean us no good. God, I thank You for a healthy and sustainable marriage.

Amen.

DAY 9: EMPOWERMENT

God is within her, she will not fall; God will help her at break of day.
- Psalm 46:5

I can't talk about Deborah without mentioning Jael, the wife of Heber the Kenite. Deborah prophesied to Barak that Sisera would be killed by a woman, which turned out to be Jael. When Sisera came to her tent, she strategically treated him respectfully, but when he asked for milk she gave him cream. He fell asleep and she killed him by driving a tent peg into his head.

What we can learn from her is empowerment, fearlessness and strategy. Sometimes, marriage can feel like a war zone. If Jael wasn't strategic, Sisera would have not been defeated. We must feel empowered to not let the enemy take our marriage when things get rough. We have to be willing to strategize by praying and fasting in order to love our husbands unconditionally and crush the head of our enemy.

How many times have we argued with our husbands and sat back waiting for him to apologize? We have got to stop waiting for our husbands to save our marriage and be empowered to do what we are supposed to do as wives. Find a prayer closet, pray to God and He will show you what to do in times of trouble. "I [God] will instruct you and teach you in the way you should go; I will counsel you with my loving eye on you" (Psalm 32:8). We picked up the wife mantle the day we said "I do". We cannot take it off. We wear it proudly, fearlessly and strategically.

Dear God,

I've been so busy finding fault with my husband that I have abandoned my responsibility as a wife, which is to nurture, honor, encourage, pray and forgive him. Forgive me for my neglect. When the enemy comes in to tear my marriage apart, give me the strength to be empowered and fearless. I will love and honor my husband and not be ashamed. I will do whatever it takes to keep my marriage. I am equipped with strength, courage and love. I am empowered.

Amen.

DAY 10:
HIS SINS

I, even I, am he who blots out your transgressions, for my own sake, and remembers your sins no more. - Isaiah 43:25

On our wedding day, ten seconds before I said "I do," I stood across from my fiancé and stared him in his misty eyes. I thought, "I am ready." I knew and understood what marriage was about to bring and I knew that there was no turning back from the good, the bad and the ugly. The ugly hit me considerably hard.

When we marry our husbands, we marry all of them, including their demons. While we can't deliver them from those things, we must allow God to use us to help our husbands. Constantly arguing with him and making him feel guilty does not aid in the deliverance process. "The Lord redeems his servants; no one will be condemned who takes refuge in him" (Psalm 34:22). Since I realized I wasn't helping my husband by condemning him, I began to ask God how I could help him. The things I wanted to complain about, I poured out to God instead and He gave me peace while reminding me that this will pass. Therefore, my husband felt comfortable sharing with me the times when he felt weak. I showed my husband the same love and compassion of God. I encouraged him and we prayed. By the strength of God, along with time and my husband's honesty, I began to love and trust my husband even more.

Dear God,

At this time, I pray that You give me peace that surpasses all understanding. I pray that You soften my heart toward my husband. I pray that You equip me with the strength and strategy that I need to love my husband and aid him in his deliverance process. Let the love, peace, guidance and agape spill from Your heart, to mine and into my husband's. I surrender all to You and I will forgive my husband of his sins.

Amen.

DAY 11: SACRIFICE

And walk in the way of love, just as Christ loved us and gave himself up for us as a fragrant offering and sacrifice to God. - Ephesians 5:2

A close friend of mine asked me, "What is the greatest lesson that marriage has taught you?" I said, "Sacrifice." I've found that selflessness in marriage can be difficult, but I'm willing to endure it because of the unconditional love I have for my husband. For example, if my husband offends me, I choose to work through it because our love, and God's ability to make all things new, is greater than any discomfort I may experience as result of my sacrifice.

Nurturing is essential in marriage. Nurturing allows us the ability to put others needs before our own. Husbands go through things mentally, spiritually and physically just like wives do. What does your husband need right now? When he upsets you, do you ever think that your husband may be battling against something?

When that happens, are you willing to set aside your own anger, hurt or disappointment so that you can save your marriage and return back to the love of Christ? I am not saying that it is our duty to heal our husband's hurt or raise them, only God can do that, but we CAN control our responses.

My favorite love scripture in the Bible I Corinthians 13:5 says, "It [love] it is not rude, it is not self-seeking, it is not easily angered, it keeps no record of wrongs." Sacrifice may not sound pretty or attractive, but the act of Christ laying down His disappointment, His hurt and His life for us is the most beautiful display of unconditional love. Imagine that in your marriage.

Dear Jesus Christ,

I thank You for sacrificing Yourself for me. I thank You for looking past my flaws and seeing me as beautiful enough to die for. Thank You for loving me. Thank You for equipping me with the ability to love my husband unconditionally. Thank You for allowing me to see my husband through Your eyes and for reminding me of the wonderful man that my husband truly is, despite the storm that he may be facing.

Amen.

DAY 12:
SELF-CARE

Rather, it should be that of your inner self, the unfading beauty of a gentle and quiet spirit, which is of great worth in God's sight.- 1Peter 3:4

Deborah wore many different hats. The Word says that she was a wife, judge, prophet, and leader. As wives, we also wear many hats. We are companions, mothers, entrepreneurs, workers, pastors, first ladies, chefs, nurturers, youth leaders, etc. Since we do many of these things and more, we can begin to feel depleted. We must remember that the most important thing that keeps us going, as wives, is God first, then self-care, which is something I can also stand to practice more.

When the prophet Elijah felt depressed and lonely, the angel of the Lord came to him and said, "Get up and eat for the journey is too much for you" (1 Kings 19:7b). It's alright to feel like you need to take rest. What do we do when our cars run out of gas? We fill it up. What if it needs maintenance? We make sure we take it to the shop to be serviced. As wives, we must do the same and make sure we're properly fed, mentally and spiritually.

I believe that Deborah's form of self-care was writing poetry. Writing poetry and journaling has also been a great outlet for me. Also, just recently, I went to get a pedicure and picked up some sexy lingerie. These things weren't only for my husband, but because they made me feel good and boosted my confidence, another act of self-care. What does self-care look like for you? Think about it and take some time out for yourself. Warriors need breaks too.

Dear God,
I just thank You for allowing me sweet rest. With all the responsibilities I have, I thank You for giving me this time to focus on me and what I enjoy. I thank You God, for being my nurturer. This is truly a time to refuel my fire for my husband. On the days where I am spinning too much, I ask that You remind me to rest, so I won't crash. Thank you for my mental stability. I am refreshed.
Amen

DAY 13: WORSHIP

My soul will boast in the Lord; let the afflicted hear and rejoice. - Psalm 34:2

Believe it or not, one of the best ways to get through our trials is to thank God. Sometimes, when we go through things, we end up feeling as flimsy as a flower after it has been stepped on. My husband and I have learned to go to God in transparency. We've shed our tears, and now it's time to thank God for the wars we've triumphed.

Deborah worshipped God through songs of praise. As a warrior, I am sure there were times when she worshipped God during the war. And, after she won the war, the entire fifth chapter of Judges notes her song of praise. What does worship look like for you? Is it journaling? Singing? Dancing? Whatever it is, remember that it breaks yokes of pain and/or bondage off you. Also, as you worship, God will begin to rebuild your confidence, first in yourself, then in your marriage.

While worshipping, you will begin to prophesy over your marriage. I am reminded of David who danced even in the storm after his son passed. "Then David got up from the ground, he went to the house of the Lord and worshipped" (2 Samuel 12: 20). He danced with all his might. Be free to worship God as you want. No restraint is needed.

Dear God,

I praise You for being the wonderful God that You are. You have consistently wrapped me in Your blanket of love and peace, in a room full of chaos. I thank God for my husband and for the mighty man of God he is. You have made me beautiful, confident and strong. You have made my husband faithful and loving. Even if You don't do another thing for me, God I give You praise.

Amen.

We Have Arrived

Together we will worship our God and King
With bowed heads and gripped hands
From our hearts, His praises we will sing

Together we will arise
Husband I am your Queen
I give God glory because you are my beautiful surprise

My protector, my provider, because of you I've survived
My love for you I surrender
Glory be to God because we have arrived!

DAY 14: COMPARISON

You shall not covet your neighbor's house. You shall not covet your neighbor's wife, or his male or female servant, his ox or donkey, or anything that belongs to your neighbor. - Exodus 20:17

How many times have we gone on Instagram and seen #relationshipgoals and said, "I wish my husband would do that?" Or how many times have we heard our girlfriends say, "My husband has never and would never do that to me?" There have been many times when I've given in to these thoughts and compared my relationship to others that I think are successful. That comparison mentally attacked me, made me think falsely of my husband and made me insecure in my marriage. I was in the perfect position for the enemy to attack me. I was too busy being against my partner because I was looking at someone else's battleground. Note I said "battleground," because nobody's relationship is perfect.

We should not compare ourselves, but rejoice with them. For instance, if I see that a wife just announced that she is pregnant and my husband and I have been struggling to get pregnant, I will say, "God, I rejoice for them. Thank You for giving them a happy healthy baby. Amen." This praise keeps you in control of what your mind thinks.

Remember that every couple has different experiences. Nobody is on the same playing field as you, except your husband. There is nothing like the bliss of being in your own world with your husband, making your own plans, going on your own dates, working out your own problems and just doing life with each other. "Do not conform to the pattern of this world, but be transformed by the renewing of your mind" (Romans 12:2a). It's about you, him and God. Stay in your lane and work on YOUR relationship.

Dear God,

Help me to not compare my marriage to others'. Remind me that I don't know everything about that couple. When I think their marriage is perfect or better than mine, help me to delight in my own marriage. Refocus my mind to create action steps that will bring our dreams to reality, not because we see another couple doing it, but because we desired it on our own. I ask that You bless that couple and pray that You give them many long years of happy matrimony. I thank You for blessing my marriage and for giving us the desires of our heart.

Amen.

DAY 15: GENDER ROLES

How good and pleasant it is when God's people live together in unity!
- Psalm 133:1

One of the most important aspects of a marriage is making sure that husband and wife are in agreement. You can't fight the enemy if you are against each other. With this being said, we know that there are specified roles in the Bible: The husband is the leader, protector, and provider. The woman's role is to help and nurture.

It is a popular belief that this means that the man is to work and the wife can work, but is not obligated to, as long as she still cooks and cleans. Well, contrary to popular belief I don't believe that this is the way that God designed marriage.

He designed marriage for us to be on one accord. If you are both in agreement that your husband cooks the meals, then so be it. If you and your husband work and you are satisfied with pulling in more money than your husband, then so be it. There are certain roles that we wives are naturally prone to do, like nurturing. For men protecting is very natural. Do not cause conflict in your marriage because of popular opinion. Again, "Do not conform to the pattern of this world, but be transformed by the renewing of your mind" (Romans 12:2).

It is not God's will that you stay in agreement with the world. However, it must be a Godly decision and founded on the biblical principles. Once I kicked other people out of my yard and found out what was acceptable to God in my marriage, I was filled with so much peace, which bought more peace and pleasure into my marriage.

Dear God,

Each season looks different in marriage. Allow me to be in agreement with my husband in this season of our lives. Allow us to not be distracted by the naysayers who are against us. Draw us to those who love us and will bring us closer together. I thank You for the peace that surrounds us.

Amen.

DAY 16:
PUTTING IN WORK

As the body without the spirit is dead, so faith without deeds is dead.
- James 2:26

My favorite poet, the late Maya Angelou, said, "You can't expect things to work if you don't work." Wives, we spend so much time pointing the finger at our husbands. Believe me, I understand that sometimes we are hurt, feel betrayed, and/or disappointed by what they have done to us. I want you to know that God has acknowledged your pain. Our husbands probably will never understand and it's not up to us to force them to. Get in your prayer closet, be transparent and let God handle it.

Although we are hurting, we must remember that our role as wife never stops. "So in everything, do to others what you would have them do to you" (Matthew 7:12a). We are called to love our husbands as Christ loves His church. Remember when we condemned Jesus and He still loved us? The same applies to our marriage. Think about this: How can we expect things to change in our marriages if we still want to show anger to our husbands?

Continuing to show love throughout the mess in your marriage is work. But, if you want your marriage to succeed, you must show love. What do you think would make him smile? Think about what you want from your husband and ask yourself if you're doing those things. Do you want a date night? You should take your husband out. Do you want a foot rub? Try rubbing his feet. Only God knows what he truly needs, so let him deal with your husband's soul while you do your part of the work.

Dear God,

I thank You for sending my husband to me. He has truly been a blessing to my life and a gift from You. Help him in the areas that need to be healed. Help me to be an aid to you first, then to him. Help me to be a good wife to him all the days of my life. I thank You for my healing and for his. We are healed and whole.
Amen.

DAY 17: DISTRACTIONS

I will meditate on your precepts and consider your ways.- Psalm 119:15

"Dear Heavenly Father, I pray that this fast would bring us closer together." Oh yes, this was my prayer to God once my husband and I decided to fast from television and social media. In my head, I figured that this fast would be a time of intimacy with my husband, and that we would just enjoy each other's company. But, nope, I was wrong.

Right in the beginning of our fast, we had several arguments. There were times when we had to separate ourselves from each other because we could not stand the sight of each other's face. I could not, for the life of me, figure out why we weren't vibing during this sacred time of fasting. Then, the Holy Spirit dropped it on me that the issue was distractions. Matthew 6:21 says, "For where your treasure is, there your heart will be also." My treasure had obviously not been with my husband, therefore our hearts were not connecting. We had been spending so much time with social media and television, that we didn't know how to function or get along together without them. The outside noise had distracted the inside of our 1 year and 8 months of marriage.

When we got this shocking revelation, we had a discussion and agreed to spend at least one hour together free of social media, television and cell phones. We also scheduled a weekly date night, even if we couldn't go out.

Remember that the enemy would love to keep you distracted in an attempt to destroy your intimacy in all areas. Wives, have a real conversation with your husband. Identify the distractions, then take action steps to eliminate them from your focus.

Dear God,

Keep the distractions out of my marriage. Route our faces to You first, then point them to both of us. Consume me with the desire to study my husband and learn his likes and dislikes, so I can be a better helpmeet. Remove the desire from me to stay updated on the latest social media post or television show. I want to value the time spent with my husband. Build a stronger bond between us. I speak

healthy disagreements, so we can discuss and correct them. I speak intimacy in all areas of our marriage.
Amen.

DAY 18: SEX

It burns like blazing fire, like a mighty flame. Many waters cannot quench love; rivers cannot sweep it away. - Song of Solomon 8:6b-7a

Now for the chapter we've all been waiting for…SEX! Sex within marriage is a beautiful representation of worship to God. Lovemaking is the closest thing to feeling the presence of God. There is absolutely nothing like it. I have been able to experience many great advantages of sex, like boosting my self-confidence. Most importantly, sex assists in bringing me closer to my husband and generating a tighter bond. The Bible speaks of husband and wife becoming one, "That is why a man leaves his father and mother and is united to his wife, and they become one flesh" (Genesis 2:24). This is also a demonstration of Godly lovemaking. With such a great blessing that God gave husband and wife, the enemy wants to tear it apart.

The enemy uses distractions to keep us from experiencing this Godly lovemaking and intimacy. There was a time that I had been really stressed out with my job. Every day I'd come home moody and depressed and it would keep me from having sex. I was taking my moodiness to the bedroom. I had to realize that a sexless marriage was not God's way. I decided to address my issues via counseling, instead of eliminating sex from my marriage.

Godly lovemaking should be a time when you and your husband are enjoying one another and de-stressing. There is no better feeling than the bliss of peace, privacy, focus and marvelously mind-blowing lovemaking between you and your husband, free of distraction.

Dear God,

Help me to address my own issues instead of bringing them into our bedroom. Father, on the days when I am not in the mood, help me by reminding me what a great, hard-working, faithful and fine man my husband is. Keep the intimacy in my marriage flowing, so that I constantly fall in love with my husband over and over again.
Amen.

DAY 19: SUBMISSION

Wives, in the same way submit yourselves to your own husbands so that, if any of them do not believe the word, they may be won over without words by the behavior of their wives. - I Peter 3:1

One thing that I can appreciate about God's design for marriage is that there is no confusion about it. Our husbands are the heads of our households, it is what it is. But what if you feel more advanced spiritually because you feel you have a stronger relationship with God and you serve the church? Or what if he just got laid off and you're still working? Do you still submit? The answer is yes.

Deborah's husband Lapidoth's name was only mentioned once. Judges, chapters 4-5, focus on Deborah and how she was a leader by occupation. Lapidoth's name means, "to fan the flame." In my eyes, that means Lapidoth encouraged her to be the best that she could be. I imagine Deborah coming home from a long day and her husband being there to inspire her and keep her light lit for her assignment. That's true love. How easy is it to submit to a man who encourages you to pursue your purpose?

Submission is about love and not about man-made rules of rank or our judgment of whether or not he is holy enough. If you find it hard to submit, look at the ways in which your husband loves and encourages you.

Dear God,

I thank You for submission. I will submit to You first and then to the wonderful man that You have given to me. I thank You for my Lapidoth. He keeps me lit and helps me to pursue my purpose. I thank You for giving me a man that loves and supports me. I am truly blessed.
Amen.

DAY 20: IMAGE

Then the Lord God made a woman from the rib he had taken out of the man, and he brought her to the man. - Genesis 2:22

As I mentioned in the previous chapter, Deborah had a husband named Lapidoth. I'm not sure about you, but every time I hear his name I associate him with Deborah and I see him as respected. Wives, ask yourself, "Is my husband respected because of me?" Even the elders respected the husband of the Proverbs 31 woman because of her image. "Her husband is respected at the city gate" (Proverbs 31:23a).

Once we got married we became one. We need to understand that whatever we do is going to be a reflection of our men. What are we saying about him in public? What are we doing in public? What are we posting on social media? When we have a fight with our husbands, do we gossip about him to our girlfriend? We are our husband's rib so that means we are part of his image.

Men love and appreciate respectable women. Lifting our husbands up is not only done when we're at home with him, but it's also how we should conduct ourselves outside of our homes. We don't want our husbands to come home embarrassed because of something we did. He deserves to be respected and honored. Understand that even in hard times, you must present him as the king of your household. He is royalty. You can't call yourself queen if you are not respecting your king. By you respecting yourself and him outside of home even when there are problems in your relationship, God will honor that and He does not forsake the righteous.

Dear God,

Cleanse me of every ill thought I have of my husband. Address me so that I am aware of my actions. Help me to be all my husband needs in and outside of our home. Show me how to be graceful, elegant and upstanding, so my husband can be viewed in the same light. He is honorable, loving, sincere and works hard for his family. Help me to show this through my actions.
Amen.

DAY 21:
FINANCES

And my God will meet all your needs according to the riches of his glory in Christ Jesus. - Philippians 4:19

According to Ramsey Solutions, finances is the second leading cause of divorce behind infidelity. This means that this is an economic demon that we wives need to defeat. Let's pull again from the other dopest wife in the Bible, the Proverbs 31 Wife. Proverbs 31:16 says, "She considers a field and buys it; out of her earnings she plants a vineyard." I love this scripture because it proves that she was a lender, not a borrower. She saw what she needed and was able to use her own money to buy it. She even had earnings to plant a vineyard.

In no way am I saying that it's wrong to take out a loan or borrow money. But, I am saying that building up your finances will create a financial freedom for your family. What I am learning in this season is the power of saving money. I am a wife who believes in multiple streams of income. It's my desire to contribute financially to my marriage. Think about what your gifts are or what you enjoy doing. Is it sewing, braiding hair or doing makeup? Whatever it is can be used as additional income to put into a savings account or for payments. Bringing something additional to the table can do nothing less than help your marriage.

Dear God,

Teach me how to be a steward of my finances. Give me the wisdom and discernment that I need in order to create and maintain financial stability in my marriage. You created me to be a helper to my husband, so teach me how to assist my husband with the finances. Stir up the creativity within me that will help me discover new ways to add to our household. Bless my hands and anoint them with oil so everything I touch will be prosperous.
Amen.

DAY 22: AFFIRM HIM

Finally, brothers, whatever is true, whatever is noble, whatever is right, whatever is pure, whatever is lovely, whatever is admirable-if anything is excellent or praiseworthy-think about such things. - Philippians 4:8

"I won't harm you with words from my mouth. I love you I need you to survive." This is one of my favorite Gospel songs by Hezekiah Walker that I relate to my husband. I am a straight to the point, sharp woman. I say what I mean and I mean what I say. But wifehood has taught me that I need to put more love in my language.

I love my husband so much and he deserves to hear me say it. Often times, when I am upset with him, I try to remember what is true about him. Usually, what comes to mind is, "My husband is a good, strong, faithful and honest man." Since I know this about him, it makes sense for me to tell him.

Rule of thumb, if you think something good about him, be sure to tell him. With everything that comes against him, you must keep him uplifted. Sometimes we don't realize our power as wives. Speak life into your husband and say what you want to see. For example, if you wish your husband would worship God more, the moment you hear him say, "Thank you, God." that is your cue to say, "Babe, it is so sexy when you thank God." Ephesians 4:29 says, "Let everything you say be good and helpful so that your words be an encouragement to those who hears them." Let your words be sweet like honey.

Dear God,

Thank You for giving me a faithful husband. I thank You for his strength and endurance. I thank You for giving him the heart to put You first. I thank You for his kindness and generosity. I thank You for his boldness and courage. I thank You for his heart of forgiveness. I thank You for his ability to stay focused and to work hard for his family. I thank You for reminding me daily to affirm my husband and my marriage. Thank You for building my marriage on a solid foundation. I thank You for breathing life and for a thriving marriage.

Amen.

DAY 23:
SWEET AS A HONEYBEE

And as she stood behind him at his feet weeping, she began to wet his feet with her tears. Then she wiped them with her hair, kissed them and poured perfume on them. - Luke 7:38

The name Deborah means "honey bee". No matter the situation, as wives we should want our husbands to feel the sweet love of Christ when they are with us. There was a woman in the Bible who dripped sweet perfume on Jesus' feet. What a lovely vision to see.

When our husbands come home, are we rubbing oils and perfumes on his feet or are we dropping hot coals on his head? My favorite First Lady, Michelle Obama, said, "When they go low, you go high." I know sometimes our husbands may say or do something that we don't like and it can cause us to want to explode, but we have to remember that we can't fight what we think is evil with evil. Pulling again from my other favorite wife in Proverbs 31, verse 12 says, "She brings him good, not harm, all the days of her life." Not one day, not when he buys her flowers, but all the days of her life.

Put on the armor of God and speak sweet or shut up. We have the power of love. The days when I can feel the smoke coming out of my ears I begin to journal. What ways can you find to help you be the sweet woman of God you are? We are wives, not wasps.

Dear God,

Help me to set the tone for my household. I declare peace, honor and respect over it. I anoint it with Your oil. When my husband walks through the door, he will immediately feel Your presence. This home will be a house of prayer, laughter, joy and comfort. Equip me to be a helpmeet to my husband when he comes home stressed and tired. Show me how to love him. Show me how to drench him in sweet honey and perfumes, in whatever area is needed. Amen.

DAY 24: FREEDOM

It is for freedom that Christ has set us free. Stand firm, then, and do not let yourselves be burdened again by a yoke of slavery.- Galatians 5:1

You have arisen! By now, you understand that you are confident and you are loved. You know the power of speaking life into your marriage and are equipped with strength! Do you believe it? No matter the circumstances, you should understand that you have won your battle. Praise be to God for freedom and maturity!

God has made you free from doubt, free from despair, free from the opinions of others and free from following the principles of this world. Wives, walk in confidence! When Deborah won the war she said, "So may all of your enemies perish, Lord! But may all who love you be like the sun when it rises in its strength" (Judges 5:31). Wives, since we have made Christ the center of our marriages, He has blessed us with unexplainable strength and faith to be able to fight for our marriages and love unconditionally.

Dear God,

Thank You for Your power of freedom. Thank You for breaking the bondage of fear, shame, doubt and selfishness off me. Thank You for reminding me that I have always been free to love my husband unconditionally. Thank You for Your Word and Your promises for my marriage. I will stand on it forever. You will always be the center of my marriage. My husband and I have risen together. Thank You.

Amen.

I See You

You, I just can't keep my eyes off you

From the first day I watched you

You released your frustration with the world

And broke free from the pain

You, you surrendered to God and let your tears flow like rain

And that day I saw you

You, a man who is not afraid to be vulnerable in the face of the Lord

A man who sings, "I'm going to run anyway," just to let your enemies know that you are still in this race

You, I just can't keep my eyes off you

I love to see you worship

You, you ignite the fire of love within me as you worship our Father

My soul gives thanks

My eyes water with joy, my soul is restored

Because I watch you, I see you

You leaning on God and leading our family

You are a man

My man

And I won't stop seeing you

Arise!: The Devotional for Warrior Wives

Photo Credit: Lamar Simms Photography

Arise!: The Devotional for Warrior Wives

www.ingramcontent.com/pod-product-compliance
Lightning Source LLC
Chambersburg PA
CBHW061511040426
42450CB00008B/1558